MW01265591

The Greek word for "life" is "Zoë." It means having a God-kind of life. Jesus came so that you would have life, and have life more abundantly.

Free

to be

Me

ZOE
HOUSE
PUBLISHERS

Zachery Tims

Free To Be Me by Zachery Tims

Published by: Zoe Publishing House
                  www.zoepublishinghouse.com

First Printing: November 2003

Scripture quotations marked KJV are taken from the Holy Bible, King James Version.

Scripture quotations marked NKJV are from the Holy Bible, New King James Copyright © 1979, 1980, 1982 by Thomas Nelson, Inc. publishers. Used by permission.

Scripture quotations marked NCV are from the Holy Bible, New Century Version Copyright © 1987, 1988, 1991 by Word Publishing, a division of Thomas Nelson Inc. Used by permission.

Scripture quotations marked NIV are from the Holy Bible, New International Version. Copyright © 1973, 1978, 1984, International Bible Society. Used by permission of Zondervon Publishing House.

International Standard Book Number: 0-9744449-0-1

01 02 03 04 05   8 7 6 5 4 3 2 1

Printed in the United States of America

Dedication

First, to the Lord Jesus Christ who, in the critical stages of my youth, delivered me from my identity crisis to lead me into my divine destiny.

To my beloved wife, Riva, who saw a distant star shining in darkness and took a chance for God's purpose to be revealed in our lives.

To my four beloved children, Zoe, Zachery III, Zahria, and Zion. The generational curse has been broken off my life and you are now blessed to walk in the legacy of divine greatness and destiny.

To Dr. Douglas ChukwuEmeka for being bold enough to be a Christian in public and for mentoring me towards my purpose to do the same. Thanks for introducing me to Jesus.

To my dedicated staff and loving members of New Destiny Christian Center who have helped to make the dream, God's plan, become a reality in me.

Thank you.

Table of Contents

Zachery Tims

Foreword

Are you one of the millions of citizens on planet Earth who live your life feeling empty and unfulfilled? Do you wonder, "What is God's will for my life?" Is your heart's cry to find your true destiny and purpose? You are not alone. Throughout the ages, humans have always been searching for themselves, for God, and for purpose.

After accepting Jesus into your life, you begin an amazing journey that ultimately ends with eternal life. Along the way, Christians develop an intense desire to serve God. Some are called to the ministry of preaching, while others are called to the ministry of helps. Most volunteer to work in the church in the nursery or in Sunday school classes, ushering, or singing. All of these things are good and need to continue. However, in serving, are you one of those who still feel unfulfilled? If so, your life is about to be revolutionized!

My friend and spiritual son, Dr. Zachery Tims, has written this book especially for you. In it, he will help you understand and identify God's perfect plan for your life so that you will inherit your perfect destiny.

Pastor Randy White

Without Walls International Church

Tampa, FL

Introduction

Everyone has a purpose, a destiny, and a calling that God has given them. In order to find these, you must first see yourself through God's eyes. When God looked at Adam, God saw the world. When God looked at Abraham, God saw the father of many nations. When God looked at Moses, God saw the deliverer of Israel. When God looked at David, God saw a king.

Would you like to know what God sees when He looks at you? You need to know that no matter who you have become or where you have been, God loves you and has a plan for your life. It is not too late to find your destiny.

Zachery Tims

CHAPTER 1

DESTINY BEFORE IDENTITY

According to Webster's dictionary, "destiny" means having a future that is predetermined. "Identity" means the fact of being the same; individuality; self. God predetermined our destiny long before we were born. However, our identity is formed through our personality and character. If destiny is predetermined, then when were our individual destinies predetermined? The Bible says that God decided upon our destinies when we were in the womb. Throughout the Bible, God shows us many people whose destinies were determined in the womb. For example, Jeremiah was destined to be a great prophet, which was a much bigger job than the man who would carry out the workload. Even before Jeremiah set foot upon the Earth, God had decided his destiny:

> *Then the word of the LORD came unto me, saying, "Before I formed thee in the belly I knew thee; and before thou camest forth out of the womb I sanctified thee, and I ordained thee a prophet unto the nations."*
> *Jeremiah 1:4-5 KJV*

In that same way, God knew you before He placed you in your mother's womb. Jeremiah's vocation and job description were decided before his birth. As He did with Jeremiah, God determined what you would do before you ever drew a breath. Before your birth, God saw something on Earth that needed to be done, and He sent you here to do it. Even if your mom or dad did not want you or plan for you, you are not an accident. God wanted you here and He used your mom and dad as the vessels to get you here. You were taken out of God's bosom and placed here in your rightful time. God has plans for you today!

Even though Jeremiah's identity, or what he thought of himself, may have been that of a child:

> *Then said I, "Ah, Lord GOD! Behold, I cannot speak: for I am a child."*
> *Jeremiah 1:6 KJV*

His destiny was that of a prophet:

> *But the LORD said unto me, "Say not, I am a child: for thou shalt go to all that I shall send thee, and whatsoever I command thee thou shalt speak. Be not afraid of their faces: for I am with thee to deliver thee, saith the Lord." Then the Lord put forth His*

hand, and touched my mouth. And the Lord said unto me, "Behold, I have put my words in thy mouth. See, I have this day set thee over the nations and over the kingdoms, to root out, and to pull down, and to destroy, and to throw down, to build, and to plant."
Jeremiah 1:7-10 KJV

Even though God called him, Jeremiah saw his identity before looking at his destiny. This is backwards. You should never place your identity before your destiny, as your identity will pervert your destiny. People tend to view their destinies through the eyes of personality and character, which have nothing to do with destiny. Often, people rely on their psyche or flesh and try to carnally discern what God has called them to do. They look at their qualifications, abilities, or inabilities instead of where God is leading them. This is a perversion of destiny because situations change; abilities and attitudes change; skills and knowledge change. As most people evolve, their tastes change. They change. But destiny remains firm. Your destiny is fixed and never sways. It is divine and eternal. Therefore, no matter how old you are, it is not too late to find your destiny.

For whom He did foreknow, He also did predestinate to be conformed to the image of his Son, that He might be the firstborn among many brethren. Romans 8:29 KJV

This Scripture clearly sets forth the notion that God has an eternal plan for your life. Throughout history, the Bible talks about many people whose destinies were determined before birth. Time after time, we see how God told parents of their children's destinies. Even before any of these children ever parted the flesh veil of their mothers' birth canals, God had determined what these children would do in life. He set the children's purposes and plans. The parents of Jacob and Esau, Samson, Solomon, John the Baptist and Jesus were all told of their children's destinies before the children were born. The parents embraced God's visions for their children and proclaimed the Lord's goodness. In Genesis, God spoke to Rebecca and revealed to her the divine destinies of her sons.

When Rebecca was pregnant with Esau and Jacob they wrestled in the womb. Rebecca wondered what was happening in her so God revealed that two nations were in her womb. Esau was born first, but Jacob was holding onto his heel trying to hold him back. Genesis 25:21-26 NKJV

While still in the womb, Jacob and Esau wrestled with each other, thus beginning to fulfill their destiny. They were two nations in the womb and that is what God saw when he looked at Esau and Jacob. God wanted there to be a separation of people, and these two children were sent to fulfill this plan. Although Esau was the firstborn and the one who was supposed to receive the blessings of God, God had already decreed that Jacob, the second born, would walk with the blessings.

Samson is another example of God's predetermined plans for our lives. Samson was a man of great strength. He was God's strong man, who was destined to lead the Israelites away from the Philistines. An angel came to Manoah and his wife to deliver God's destiny plans to them about their son Samson. The Lord revealed very detailed instructions to them regarding what God had in store for Samson. He told them they would have a son and that they were to set him apart so he would become a Nazarite. God instructed them that their child must not indulge in wine, strong drink or put a razor to his head. The Lord continued and said that Samson would be a great warrior of Israel and would deliver the Israelites from the Philistines who had been oppressing them. God saw a need and sent Samson here to fulfill the need. By putting Samson in this position, God was going to get the glory. Samson was just the tool that God used.

Now there was a certain man from Zorah, of the family of the Danites, whose name was Manoah; and his wife was barren. And the Angel of the Lord appeared to the woman and said to her, "Indeed now, you are barren and have borne no children, but you shall conceive and bear a son. Now therefore, please be careful not to drink wine or similar drink, and not to eat anything unclean. For behold, you shall conceive and bear a son. And no razor shall come upon his head, for the child shall be a

Nazarite to God from the womb; and he shall begin to deliver Israel out of the hand of the Philistines." Judges 13:2-5 NKJV

David was a man after God's own heart. David worshiped God in the good times and in the bad times. True, David made some serious mistakes when he slept with Bathsheba, another man's wife. David's sin multiplied when Bathsheba became pregnant and David had her husband killed. Additionally, the baby died. But David continued to worship God. After David married Bathsheba, she became pregnant again. And God did something very interesting. God spoke about the baby before the baby was born. God began talking about Solomon. God told David that David's heir would build a place where God would again establish His kingdom.

When your days are fulfilled and you rest with your fathers, I will set up your seed

*after you, who will come from your body,
and I will establish his kingdom. He shall
build a house for My name, and I will
establish the throne of his kingdom forever.
I will be his Father, and he shall be My son.
If he commits iniquity, I will chasten him
with the rod of men and with the blows of
the sons of men. But My mercy shall not
depart from him, as I took it from Saul,
whom I removed from before you. And your
house and your kingdom shall be
established forever before you. Your throne
shall be established forever.*
2 Samuel 7:12-16 NKJV

Again, God saw a need concerning the rebuilding of
the temple. God's plan was for the temple to be
constructed to honor Him. So God created Solomon
as the man for the job.

In another example, John the Baptist was proclaimed to be the forerunner of Jesus Christ. Even before John was conceived, an angel appeared to John's father and talked about the kind man John would become. The angel said John would make a way in the wilderness and the spirit of Elijah would rest upon him.

Then an angel of the Lord appeared to him, standing on the right side of the altar of incense. And when Zacharias saw him, he was troubled, and fear fell upon him. But the angel said to him, "Do not be afraid, Zacharias, for your prayer is heard; and your wife Elizabeth will bear you a son, and you shall call his name John. And you will have joy and gladness, and many will rejoice at his birth. For he will be great in the sight of the Lord, and shall drink neither wine nor strong drink. He will also be filled with the Holy Spirit, even from his mother's womb. And he will turn many of the children of Israel to the Lord their God. He will also go before Him in the spirit and power of Elijah, 'to turn the hearts of the fathers to the children,' and the disobedient to the wisdom of the just, to make ready a people prepared for the Lord."

Luke 1:11-17 NKJV

Now, John the Baptist's father did not embrace what the angel of the Lord told him about his son. Why should he? In the natural, Zacharias knew that he was old and his wife, Elizabeth, was also along in years and barren. Zacharias looked at himself and the identity of his wife, Elizabeth. He did not see the destiny for himself, Elizabeth, or even his son. Thankfully, Zacharias' view did not deter God's purpose. God would not be stopped even though Zacharias was full of disbelief. In order for Zacharias to stop doubting, God had to do something drastic. So, God took away Zacharias' speech until John was born. John was the one chosen to forge the path for Jesus. You could say John was God's voice in the wilderness.

Jesus' destiny is told throughout the Old Testament. You can find hundreds of prophecies concerning Jesus Christ. A striking prophecy was given to a young girl, a virgin about fourteen years old. She was told that the Savior of the world would be conceived in her womb and that she would become the mother of the Messiah. She was told that the Savior was coming.

Now in the sixth month the angel Gabriel was sent by God to a city of Galilee named Nazareth, to a virgin betrothed to a man whose name was Joseph, of the house of David. The virgin's name was Mary. And

*having come in, the angel said to her,
"Rejoice, highly favored one, the Lord is
with you; blessed are you among women!"
But when she saw him, she was troubled at
his saying, and considered what manner of
greeting this was. Then the angel said to
her, "Do not be afraid, Mary, for you have
found favor with God. And behold, you will
conceive in your womb and bring forth a
Son, and shall call His name JESUS. He
will be great, and will be called the Son of
the Highest; and the Lord God will give
Him the throne of His father David. And He
will reign over the house of Jacob forever,
and of His kingdom there will be no end."
Luke 1:26-29 NKJV*

Jesus Christ was God's ultimate sacrifice for the
world. God sent Him down to earth as the perfect
sacrifice for our sins. He died so that all men could

live. Even Jesus had a destiny. Like all the men previously mentioned, your identity is caught up in God. Your destiny is not in what you wear, where you live, whom you marry, or what others say about you. Your identity is in God and is directly tied to your destiny in Him. Your destiny should mold your identity because your destiny existed long before your identity and will outlive your identity.

Destiny Means Having A Purpose

We came out of God for a purpose. Finding your destiny means having a purpose. In fact, everyone has a purpose. The trick is finding God's purpose for your life. We do not decide our destiny. That is up to God. Before Jeremiah ever had a name, he had a predetermined purpose. The same is true for us. God has decided our purposes and He wants us to discover it and fulfill it. Do not get discouraged while you are trying to find your purpose in life. Never tell God what you cannot do because in Him you can do all things. The fact that God sent you here is proof that you can do whatever God asks you to do. God will not ask you to do something He knows you are unable to do. You may think the task is impossible. However, the reality is that it has already been done in God's mind and He desires for you to do it. Pursuing your destiny means functioning in the realm of your calling. Whatever God tells or asks you to do, you are able to do. He will empower you to do it.

I can do all things through Christ which strengtheneth me. Philippians 4:13 KJV

There is a grace that God will impart to you that will make what you do look easy. That ease is the sign God gives you as proof of, or evidence of, your calling. This means what would take others a week to do, you can do in minutes. It is a God-given ability inspired by God. It is not merely a talent. It is an outlet where God steps in and miraculously demonstrates His power in your human effort.

My wife, for example, does not like to preach. She does not want to preach. When she is asked to preach, she locks herself in a room and tells me to leave her alone. What easily takes me minutes to do can take her weeks. So, I take care of the kids while she is in the Word, preparing a message, and occupying the computer. She does, however, have a grace to exhort. She can open up the heavens in a matter of minutes. My wife has the gifting to exhort in a way I cannot. She can take the microphone, not knowing exactly what to say, and then beautifully and effortlessly uplift the church congregation on the spot! And that is what I am talking about. Pursuing your destiny means that your calling will flow in a manner that appears effortless.

Simply because someone else operates so easily in their calling does not give us license to get jealous of their calling or destiny. It is very easy to be jealous of someone else's destiny. You may think that the destiny God wants for you is inferior or not as good as someone else's destiny. That thinking is wrong and dangerous. Never think that your destiny is not as good as someone else's destiny. God has chosen you to do something that only you can do for Him. So do it with excellence and He will bless you.

In Chapters 25 through 31 of the Book of Exodus, God told Moses to take an offering from the people before the Tabernacle was constructed. They were to bring the materials that would be fashioned into the mercy seat, table of incense, and all the instruments of the Outer Court, Holy Place, and Holy of Holies. God named two men that He ordained to be the chief engineers or head craftsmen. Those men were not called to preach. Yet, what they were called to do was just as important. We cannot all be the head. Some of us are called to fulfill other destinies. No matter what destiny God has called you to, remember He ordained it for you.

Whom Do You Identify With?

Proverbs 23:7 declares, "As a man thinketh so is he," or so he becomes. At the age of twelve, I became involved with the wrong people. I did not know anything about destiny, let alone my own destiny. My parents went to church, but they had no real spiritual connection to the Kingdom of God. I thought it was cool to wear Air-Jordans, puff football coats, and lambskins. I related to that style even though most of the people who dressed that way were drug dealers. Since I identified with drug dealers through fashion and what they were doing, I naturally became a drug dealer. I sought my identity with them. So I began to participate in the same activities as the drug dealers. This decision began to pervert my destiny because my identity, not my destiny, was pushing me. I was searching to fit in and any group that would receive me was okay. The brutal consequence was that my identity led me to jail at age fifteen.

Most people try looking for their identity before they discover their destiny. When looking for their identity, people seek out what they identify with just as I did. Usually, these are external things. In my case, I identified with clothing. Many times, people will connect with a look they think is cool, just as I did. Instead of valuing internal things, they value external things. However, destiny is internal, not external. Therefore, purpose and destiny can only be discerned through the Spirit. Identifying with external things causes us to listen to the opinions of people and conversely we *let them* shape our identity and direct our destiny.

A good example of this can be found in your children. They are going along in life just fine, with normal hairdos and clothes. Then suddenly they connect with a bad influence and come home with spikes in their hair and body piercing in places that you did not even know could be pierced. What happened? Where is the sweet innocent child who once lived in your house? That same child who used to dress normally found that they identified with someone else externally and they wanted an identity that was related to the other person. The reason they identified with someone else is proof of their own inner search for identity. What we need to understand is that identity does not come from outward appearances. It comes from knowing who you are, not what you have become. Your purpose is wrapped up in your destiny, not your external or outward appearance.

Most people miss it when it comes to outward appearances. We tend to dress according to trends and peer influence. I have often wondered who or what determines the trends and where the trends originate. What I have found is that music tends to contribute to fashion trends, as do high-profile personalities. Think about it. Back in the '70s, platform shoes and bell-bottom pants were all the rage. Once that trend was over, you probably gave away your platforms, bell-bottoms, and psychedelic shirts. But thirty years later, those clothes are once again in fashion. Now to be stylish, you have to go out and buy a whole new wardrobe. Tremendous amounts of money are spent on fashion every year. But fashion is only external and changes.

Searching for acceptance is not just something that plagues the young. Some adults are still searching for acceptance well after adolescence. For some women, finding a man is a high priority. They hear and believe lies such as, "you are nobody until you have a man." Some men think along similar lines. Those men believe they have to have a trophy who can be shown off. This can lead to an identity crisis.

Often, a mid-life crisis is an identity crisis. For example, consider the 50-year-old man who desires a 20-year-old girlfriend or wife. The reality behind a some relationships like that is simple. Most times, the older man is searching for a youthful, younger identity because that makes him feel good. The young girlfriend or young wife makes the older man feel younger.

Searching for what feels good now can sometimes lead to unforeseen consequences down the road. For example, in a search for what feels good, we could get consumed by material possessions or earthly titles and power. We must realize that those things do not matter. The only thing that matters is finding what God wants us to do. You must discover God's purpose and destiny for your life. When you do, PURSUE IT WITH ALL YOU HAVE!

See yourself the way God sees you. It does not matter what you wear or how you talk. You are what God wants regardless of your height, weight, age, looks, appeal or skin color. God loves you just the way you are right now. Remember, God knew you before you were in your mother's womb. Therefore, do not allow other people's opinions shape your identity and ultimately direct your destiny.

Identity is External And Destiny Is Internal

Let me explain this statement. Have you ever envied a person for their car, their house, their fashion sense, or their occupation so much that you became envious and desired their possessions? You go to college, get a degree, and acquire a coveted job only to realize that you hate it. Something is still missing. You thought that possessions or a job title was just what you wanted and would make you happy.

However, you realized that you were gravely disappointed by what you became. Why is that? Simply put, your decision was based on an outward motivation. You were motivated by what you saw and heard from the people around you. You made a destiny decision based on the external appearance of others. Always remember that your identity is based on external features while your destiny is based on internal features. Your destiny came before your identity and takes priority over your identity. Consider Samson, John the Baptist, Jesus, and Paul. Like the other examples previously mentioned, all of them all had a prophetic destiny. Scripture says that Paul was called to be an apostle from his mother's womb. In his search for an identity, Paul traveled the wrong road. Thankfully, God's plan for Paul could not be thwarted. In Chapter 9 of the Book of Acts, Paul was on the road to Damascus to persecute

Christians. On the way, he had a supernatural encounter. A bright light shone around him, knocking him to the ground. God blinded Paul so he would stop looking outwardly and start looking inwardly. Although Paul identified with the Pharisees and their external religion and religious titles, he still had to see his destiny. Though Paul was close to his purpose, he was still way off course. Blind and knocked from his beast, God told him to go to the city and shut himself in, and then Paul would begin to see his destiny. Paul had been searching his entire life to find himself, but he was looking with the wrong eyes. Now he could see with the right ones. He learned to walk by faith, not by sight. At the same time that God was dealing with Paul, He was dealing with someone else:

And there was a certain disciple at Damascus, named Ananias; and to him said the Lord in a vision, Ananias. And he said, Behold, I am here, Lord. And the Lord said unto him, Arise, and go into the street which is called Straight, and enquire in the house of Judas for one called Saul, of Tarsus: for, behold, he prayeth, And hath seen in a vision a man named Ananias coming in, and putting his hand on him, that he might receive his sight. Then Ananias answered, Lord, I have heard by many of this man, how much evil he hath done to thy saints at Jerusalem: And here he hath authority from the chief priests to bind all that call on thy name. But the Lord said unto him, Go thy way: for he is a chosen vessel unto me, to bear my name before the Gentiles, and kings, and the children of Israel: For I will shew him how great things he must suffer for my name's sake. Acts 9:10-16 KJV

Confused, Ananias probably thought the Lord was mistaken. He probably wondered when and why God chose Paul. He probably wondered if God could change a person's destiny in mid-life. Like Jeremiah was chosen, Paul was chosen from the womb. However, Paul took the wrong path. But once he had an encounter with God, Paul saw that God had called and ordained him to be God's voice in writing the New Testament. Before his birth, Paul was chosen to bring revelation knowledge. But Paul's destiny was almost perverted while he walked in darkness, chasing an identity. Only when Paul switched the two and got the order straight, did he walk into his destiny. The same Paul who used to kill and persecute Christians wrote:

But when it pleased God, who separated me from my mother's womb, and called me by his grace . . . . Galatians 1:15 KJV

Being a Pharisee, or scribe, reflected Paul's identity. But being an apostle reflected Paul's destiny. Paul distinguished between his identity and destiny by saying that he did not have to be a Pharisee to achieve what God called him to do. He was required to be an apostle because that was his destiny.

Like Paul, you can be chosen for one destiny and yet go down the wrong path. But like God did for Paul, God can open your eyes so that you can discover, live, and fulfill your destiny.

CHAPTER 2

LET GOD SHAPE YOUR IDENTITY AND DIRECT YOUR DESTINY

Do you know what God thinks when He thinks about you? Have you asked Him? If so, did you listen to His response? Or did you fix your attention on the opinions of people and allow them to dictate your destiny? Often, we are too eager to listen to people, rather than God. In the long run, we end up with displaced priorities. Chances are, you can think back to a decision you made and find that someone pressured you to do it. For some people, that type of peer pressure results in an unwanted child, an abusive relationship, a stress-filled job, or a poor financial investment. We all make the wrong choices in life at times. But we need to recognize our mistakes and repent and, with God's guidance, change. Hopefully, we will learn from our bad choices and mistakes so that the next time we have to make choices, we will make the right decision – God's decision – for our lives.

Are you beginning to find that you are guilty of obsessing about others' opinions? Do you want to look nice so that others will want to be around you? Have you ever been late for church because you had "nothing to wear," though you had your Friday night outfit dry cleaned and pressed by the Wednesday before? We have all been guilty of such things. In fact, it is normal for you to be self-conscious when being around other people. Everyone suffers from it.

Teenagers struggle with peer pressure. Often, you will see your teen in their bedroom trying on numerous outfits just so they will wear the right clothes to be accepted. A sense of belonging is just as important to them as being able to wear the right clothes and say the right things. Everyone wants to be cool or be accepted.

The reason advertisers spend millions of dollars to get you to pay attention to your appearance is that it has been proven that other people's opinions influence you. But sometimes, other people's opinions will push you in the wrong direction. Sometimes those opinions will lead you to an extremely miserable life of overindulging in every aspect of your life. Chasing after your identity can steer you off course and put you on a different road than the one God wants for you. Instead of chasing an identity, you really need to chase destiny and strive to be the person God envisioned. God created you to be an individual who would walk towards and in God's divine purpose. So give yourself some credit for the talent and destiny inside you. After all that is what really counts.

God knows the spirit part of you. He knows the real you – the one who is not fake, phony, or hypocritical. God sees you before you put on the facade. He commissioned you. He predestined you. He planned your destiny before your identity. Allow God to shape your identity and lead you to your destiny. When you know you are walking in God's destiny for your life, then you can walk confidently because you know He will be there with you every step of the way. Ultimately, His influence will directly affect your quest to reach your destiny. David's anointing as king of Israel is an example of God's influence affecting destiny.

Now the Lord said unto Samuel, How long wilt thou mourn for Saul, seeing I have rejected him from reigning over Israel? Fill thine horn with oil, and go, I will send thee to Jesse the Bethlehemite: for I have provided me a king among his sons...and thou shalt anoint unto me him whom I name unto thee. And Samuel did that which the Lord spake, and came to Bethlehem.... And he sanctified Jesse and his sons, and called them to the sacrifice. And it came to pass, when they were come, that he looked on Eliab, and said, Surely the Lord's anointed is before him. But the Lord said unto Samuel, Look not on his countenance, or on the height of his stature; because I have refused him: for the Lord seeth not as man seeth; for man looketh on the outward appearance, but the Lord looketh on the heart....Again, Jesse made seven of his sons to pass before Samuel. And Samuel said unto Jesse, The Lord hath not chosen these. And Samuel said unto Jesse, Are here all thy children? And he said, There remaineth yet the youngest, and, behold, he keepeth the sheep. And Samuel said unto Jesse, Send and fetch him: for we will not sit down till he come hither. 1 Samuel 16:1-11 NKJV

Once Samuel arrived at Jesse's house, Samuel looked upon Jesse's eldest son, Eliab, and thought that Eliab should be king. But God told Samuel otherwise. Samuel made the same mistake most us make in our decision-making tasks. How many times have we approved of someone or chose them simply based upon their external, or physical, appearance? Even David's father, Jesse, thought David was the least likely of his sons to be chosen as king. David was an outdoors boy who herded sheep all day. He did not have the stately, royal appearance his brothers possessed. David was not even present when Samuel arrived. However, Samuel told Jesse to bring forth David.

So he sent and brought him in. Now he was ruddy, with bright eyes, and good looking. And the Lord said, Arise, anoint him: for this is the one. Then Samuel took the horn of oil and anointed him in the midst of his brothers; and the Spirit of the Lord came upon David from that day forward. So Samuel rose up, and went to Ramah.
1 Samuel 16:12-13 NKJV

When God chose David as king, God did not see David's identity as a shepherd boy. God saw David's destiny.

Mistaken Identity Corrupts Perfect Destiny

Mistaken identity happens a lot. You judge a person by their clothes, car, or house. Judging a person or situation like that is risky. For example, the Israelites thought the Canaanites, Amalekites, Amorites, Hittites, and Jebusites saw them in the same way the Israelites saw themselves – as grasshoppers.

And there we saw the giants, the sons of Anak, which come of the giants: and we were in our own sight as grasshoppers, and so we were in their sight.
Numbers 13:33 KJV

The Israelites were God's chosen people. So He empowered them to conquer and occupy the Promised Land. However, ten of the twelve spies sent to survey the land returned with a bad report. The spies believed the Israelites were as small as grasshoppers. They saw themselves as being defeated. Their wrong perception led to a mistaken identity, which corrupted their destiny. The children of Israel nearly forfeited their destiny because of mistaken identity.

On the other hand, the Book of Joshua shows how all the other nations perceived the Israelites as great warriors who were mighty in battle because their God parted the Red Sea. Their enemies were in fact afraid of the Israelites; they shut down their cities, locked the gates, put spies on the walls, and refused to let in the Israelites. Even though the Israelites were mighty warriors and strong in battle, they misidentified themselves as weak and defeated before they even attempted to possess the land.

Even today, we act like the Israelites. We look at ourselves through our own eyes and often see weak, defeated people. We let the devil tell us that we are not worthy. We have a pity party and then wonder how God could ever use us because of our unworthiness. Remember Jeremiah? Jeremiah thought he was unworthy to be God's prophet when he mistook his identity for his destiny. Jeremiah saw only a child. But God saw a prophet.

When identifying ourselves, we must look beyond our outer appearance and see what is inside us. We must stand strong and accept what God says about us. God knew you were messed up before He called you. No one is perfect. God called you despite your current fleshly condition. Your destiny has nothing to do with you winning a popularity contest with God. Plain and simple, you cannot impress God. His mind was made up about you long before you were born. God loves you and wants only the best for you.

Once you realize your destiny, stay focused. Avoid listening to others' opinions. When the twelve spies came back into the Israelites' camp, the spies told everyone that they saw themselves as grasshoppers. The people in the camp accepted the misidentification and started believing that they were like grasshoppers! They probably started to think of themselves as small and insignificant. How ridiculous! How could they have accepted what others were thinking about them?

But we do the same thing! We fabricate elaborate scenarios and place ourselves in the center and then visualize everyone around us pointing fingers and shaking their heads. We need to start listening to God's voice and not the voices of others. Let God reveal your identity and your destiny.

Letting others define your destiny can be dangerous and can sway your course. Consider the story about Ananias. Ananias thought Paul was a tyrant because Paul killed Christians in the Book of Acts. Ananias was judging Paul's actions and by doing so Ananias easily could have altered the destiny that God had planned for Paul. Nevertheless, Paul realized that he was God's chosen vessel and knew that he would bear witness of God's name and glory to the Gentiles.

For I know the thoughts that I think toward

*you, saith the LORD, thoughts of peace, and
not of evil, to give you an expected end.
Jeremiah 29:11 KJV*

God preordained a place for Paul and He has
preordained a place for you. It is your purpose and
destiny. When you know your destiny, you know
there are certain things God is going to do for you
that will directly affect your destiny.

Battling God's Will Versus Your Will

Examine yourself and ask God how you got here.
What is your destiny? Are you in church because
God wants you to be there or because you are trying
to fit in? Is your job an identity source or a destiny
server? Are you married to your spouse because they
are part of your destiny or because you are trying to
create an identity? Is it God's will or your will? The

answer to all of the above questions should not center around your identity, but around God's will for your life. Often, we tend to make this harder than it really is. Remember that God foreknew you, your gifts, and your abilities. He destined you and gave you a calling before you had an identity.

The blessings you are looking to God for may not be the same blessings He desires to give you. His will and your will may be at odds. You may not even like the path God has prepared for you. It may not be what you had in mind for your life. So what happens is our carnal, fleshly side will doubt God and underestimate Him. This can make you second-guess yourself and, even worse, second-guess God. Your spirit, though, will trust God no matter what. There begins a struggle that goes on inside of you and that battle is over comfort. Your flesh wants to be in the comfort zone. Being in the comfort zone means you want to rely on things you can see, hear, taste, smell, and touch. You want proof and you want evidence. You want everything on the table all at once. But life does not work like that and wanting things based on your carnal nature is very dangerous.

Humans almost always look at the outward appearance and then make snap judgments on how to handle a situation. We need to start looking at situations the way God looks at them. We need to be sensitive to His Spirit. Do not be afraid to ask God what to do. He knows the answer even before you ask. But maybe you do not know how to achieve what God wants you to do.

The following story is about a boy who thought there was no answer. "Eldon! Come here!" His heart pounding, Eldon ran toward the shout. He wondered what his stepfather could want now. His mind raced to find an answer. Had he forgotten to do something his stepfather had commanded him to do? Or would this be an imaginary infraction and just another excuse for his stepfather to beat him? "Get in here!" his stepfather yelled. "Someone here to see you!"

When Eldon reached the front room, he saw a stranger standing by the door. Eldon had no idea who the man was or what the man wanted from him. The stranger greeted Eldon and began telling him about a special program for boys like him. He had heard about Eldon from his teacher and was interested in getting him enrolled in their afternoon sessions. They wanted to begin teaching him how to write computer software programs. Eldon's head was spinning. No one, not even member of his family, knew that Eldon's secret dream was to get a degree in software engineering.

Eldon's teacher was able to look beyond outward appearances and see what was inside. God loved Eldon so much that He sent someone to help out the young boy. That man had heard about Eldon and was sensitive to his needs and wanted to help him achieve his destiny. God can and will work miracles on our behalf. Sometimes He will give us a little nudge in the right direction because He wants us to fulfill our destinies.

Zachery Tims

CHAPTER 3

YOUR IDENTITY SHOULD NOT DESTROY YOUR DESTINY

Today's culture has conditioned us to identify with movie stars and sports figures. They are in the public eye so much that advertisers want and need them to sell their products. In fact, some stars and sports figures now have their own clothing lines, perfume or make-up. I used to identify with players for the Washington Redskins and Dallas Cowboys. I loved wearing their NFL puff jackets and lambskin coats. Everyone I knew in my neighborhood identified with the same things. In fact, unless you joined in with the gang members and began to wear the same identifying "colors," you stood to lose. My misidentification with external appearances began to resonate within the realm of my soul. I had to talk, walk, and look a certain way. I wore what they wore. I did what they did. I lived a gang banger's life. But my life was a mess. I began to sell drugs at age twelve. By age fifteen, I was deep enough into drug dealing that I started carrying a gun. As a result of identifying with drug dealers and leading that lifestyle, I had been shot at, hemmed up in hallways, held up, and jacked up.

When I was sixteen, I shot a man and tried to kill him. I remember pointing the gun at him and emptying every round – about five or six bullets. But by the grace of God, only one bullet hit him in the ankle. His injury was not fatal. Otherwise, I would still be in jail today. I was worthless and of no benefit to my family, society, or myself. My identity was wrapped up and tied to the wrong people. My way of thinking back then was based on the drug culture with which I identified. Not only did I not understand my destiny, but I also only saw my destiny and identity as the same thing. This thinking was destroying me. In all honesty, I should have been dead before I met Jesus. However, by the grace of God and His infinite plan with His all-seeing eyes and for His purpose, God kept me alive.

I thank God for His mercy. Even when I was not born again, He knew my destiny and was working for me, preserving my life so that I could fulfill my destiny for His glory! I am not the only one God has kept alive. God has kept you alive, too, so that you can fulfill the destiny God planned for you!

What People Say Has an Impact! Be Careful Whom You Listen To!

Have you ever been around someone who looks at life negatively? They are always complaining about everything and people hate to be around them because nothing is ever good enough. I do not like negativity. I do not focus on the negative side of things because I am trying with all my strength to trust God. Negative thinking makes it hard for me to keep my focus and trust God and I am trying to be more spiritual than fleshly. So rather than listen to all the ins and outs, and ups and downs of negativity, I only want to hear the bottom line.

Words can do two things. They can edify and they can destroy. You have the power of life and death in your words. Be careful how you use them. Likewise, be careful of those things you hear also. For example, consider the damage done to a child when a parent tells the child that she is "dumb" or "stupid." The child will soon believe that she is dumb and stupid. Unfortunately, this is how insecurities develop.

The right word spoken at the right time is as beautiful as gold apples in a silver bowl. Proverbs 25:11 NCV

Have you ever thought that someone did not like you, but when you were finally able to talk to them you discovered it was nothing? Thinking that others do not like you usually comes from the fact that you do not like yourself. Often, you see something in yourself that is missing or needs perfecting and think others see it as well. But they do not see the problem or know what is going on with you. You may think you eat too much or that you are too opinionated. You might think you are too fat or too skinny. Maybe your negative views force you to always see the glass half empty instead of half full.

Frankly, most people have too many problems of their own to be thinking about liking or disliking you. First and foremost, you must like yourself, and be careful to whom you listen! What people say will influence your self-perception and help direct the decisions that you will ultimately make.

Other people's opinions about you do not matter to God. So those opinions should not matter to you. You need to put aside the old self and tune into God's frequency. God is always in tune with His children. God always talks to us. At times, though, you may not hear Him. You block out God's voice when you stray from Him. When you stray from God, you end up listening to the wrong voice. It may be the voice of co-workers, gossipers, family, people from your past or even bad childhood experiences. Realize that those voices are only distractions. All that garbage taints the clarity of God's voice. Once you can hear God's voice, please understand that you are listening to God, who is guiding you to your destiny. Only you get to chose to whom you listen. Chose wisely!

CHAPTER 4

Do You Have A David Or An Eliab?

The army of Israel was at war with the Philistines when a standoff occurred. Facing each other across a valley, the Philistines had set their champion warrior, Goliath, before Israel as a challenge. Goliath bid anyone to come and fight him – one-on-one, winner take all. Every soldier in Israel heard Goliath's challenge. None, however, were brave enough to accept, except David.

And Eliab his eldest brother heard when he spake unto the men; and Eliab's anger was kindled against David, and he said, Why camest thou down hither? and with whom hast thou left those few sheep in the wilderness? I know thy pride, and the naughtiness of thine heart; for thou art come down that thou mightest see the battle. And David said, What have I now done? Is there not a cause? 1 Samuel 17:28-29 KJV

Eliab's anger was kindled against David because David had come to the battle field. Eliab's implication was that this battle was for real men and David was just a boy. Nonetheless, when Goliath taunted the children of Israel, all the mighty men were frightened, even Eliab. Only David was not troubled. The problem in Jesse's house was that everyone looked upon David as an insignificant young boy who was only good for tending a few sheep and delivering cheese and wine to the men in battle. However, God's view was completely different. David had stolen God's heart and became the apple of God's eye. God saw David as a king, a leader, and a man after His own heart. God had an obsession with David and no one even knew. David's father, Jesse, was clueless because he never asked God about his son's heart. Instead, Jesse gave David an identity that fit Jesse's agenda, which was to get someone to take care of the sheep.

Parents, this is a common error we make when we expect our children to be our housekeepers, baby-sitters, and errand runners. We stand in jeopardy of becoming self-serving in what we want them to do instead of asking God what He wants them to do. Maybe they need to spend all that baby-sitting time playing the piano or learning voice. If God told you that, would it be too much of an inconvenience? We are talking about destiny. If you keep your children in the house, controlling every move they make, never letting them express their creative abilities, they will relate to something for which they were never destined. You must let your children express the purpose and plan of God's heart for them.

Do You See What God Sees?

God sees things deep within you that others cannot see. The Bible says the Spirit searches the deep things of God.

> *But God has revealed them to us through his Spirit. 2 Corinthians 2:10 NKJV*

Destiny is deeper than what you can see with the naked eye. When God looks at you, He sees things that everyone else ignores. You are a treasure to Him in an earthly vessel. The word "treasure" means, "priceless content." Our bodies are earthen vessels in which priceless contents are placed. Your priceless contents are those things to which God is committed. They are valuable because they represent God.

But we have this treasure in earthen vessels, that the excellency of the power may be of God, and not of us. 2 Corinthians 4:7 KJV

Consider an apple. If you decide to eat it, all you have is an apple. On the other hand, if you cut the apple open, or leave it outside to decay and break down, you will discover the real power source of the apple. The power source is not on the outside. In fact, you cannot even see the power source until you get down to the core and find the seed. Yet, the shell of the seed is not the power source of the apple. It, too, must decompose, revealing the inside of the seed that has the power to reproduce.

Ask yourself what God sees when He looks upon you? Do you see yourself the way God does? Our God focuses on our positive habits and characteristics. But people will tend to focus on our negative habits and characteristics. God does not see a crippled, weak person. He only sees the potential that is inside you. It does not matter whether you are black or white, male or female, tall or short, have long or short hair, mustache or are clean-shaven, wear designer clothes or torn T-shirts. When God looks on you, He sees that person of greatness that is within you. Do you talk down about yourself? Are you always talking yourself out of stepping out and walking in faith? Do you talk yourself out of something you know you are meant to do? Do you have trouble with the spirit of procrastination? If so, then STOP! Stop being a doubter and see yourself through the eyes of God. Do not second-guess and question what God is leading you to do. That is a sign of low self-esteem. God's heart is grieved because, when He asked you to do something, you second-guessed Him and, in turn, questioned your own ability. You have very likely missed so many blessings because you see yourself as a grasshopper, just as the Israelites. It is time to start walking in your destiny. Take the limits off God and step out of your comfort zone. You can open that business. You can write that book. You can be a successful stockbroker. You can be the best mom or dad you could have ever imagined! You can do it through Christ who strengthens you!

Death Comes Before Life

Every person has two sides. One is pregnant with destiny, while the other is trapped in identity. The story of Dr. Jekyll and Mr. Hyde talks about one man being good and the other man evil. We all battle good and evil. In Romans, Paul declared:

For the good that I would I do not: but the evil which I would not, that I do. Now if I do that I would not, it is no more I that do it, but sin that dwelleth in me. I find then a law, that, when I would do good, evil is present with me. Romans 7:19-21 KJV

This dark, evil nature was passed through Adam when he broke his covenant with God. Through this transgression, we inherited that nature and it is called sin. This "human nature" is a part of us and we do not have to work to develop it. It is just there. My wife and I did not teach our children how to trick others or manipulate one parent against the other. It is product of their nature. Both good and evil are already in you. That is why a death must occur before you can really begin to live and walk in God's grace and glory. Please understand that I am not literally speaking of dying on a cross. Thankfully, Jesus already did that. I am talking about dying to your fleshly desires. This principle is illustrated in the covenant between God and Abram.

Then Abram bowed face down on the ground. God said to him, "I am making my agreement with you: I will make you a father of many nations. I am changing your name from Abram to Abraham because I am making you a father of many nations. I will give you many decedents. New nations will be born from you, and kings will come from you. And I will make an agreement between me and you and all your descendants from now on: I will be your descendants from now on: I will be your God and the God of all your descendants."

Then God said to Abraham, "You and your descendants must keep this agreement from now on. This is my agreement with you and all your descendants, which you must obey: Every male among you must be circumcised. Cut away your foreskin to show that you are prepared to follow the agreement between me and you. From now on when a baby boy is eight days old, you will circumcise him. This includes any boy born among your people or any who is your slave who is not one of your descendants."

Genesis 17:3-12 NKJV

God told Abram to cut away the foreskin of every male in his house and every male child on the eighth day. God also told Abram that because of this covenant, his name would no longer be Abram, but would be Abraham. The person who gets the calling and promise from God will not be the same person who gives it birth; a death must first take place. In Abraham's case, cutting away the flesh symbolized such death.

As previously stated, God, in Genesis, revealed to Rebecca that two nations were in her womb. The younger of her two children was Jacob, which in Hebrew means "trickster." In addition to being a trickster, Jacob was a master manipulator. Jacob was slick. He was a good salesman. He could sell ice to an Eskimo. Despite all that and despite being the youngest of the twins, God said Jacob would rule.

In Genesis 32:22-31, Jacob wrestled with a man. While they were struggling, the man touched the hollow of Jacob's hip causing Jacob to become crippled. The Bible says that Jacob refused to let the man go until the man blessed him. The man told

79

Jacob that from then on, Jacob would be called "Israel," which means "Prince of God." Jacob had to go through a maturing process, a cutting away process, or a death, before he realized his purpose. Remember the destiny God had for the apostle Paul. Before Paul realized his destiny, he was Saul of Tarsus, a well-known persecutor of Christians. In order for Saul to become fully aware of his true destiny, a death had to take place in Saul. The Saul who met God on the road to Damascus was not the same Saul when the encounter ended. Even his name was changed to Paul. Afterwards, Paul said,

I am crucified with Christ: nevertheless I live; yet not I, but Christ liveth in me: and the life which I now live in the flesh I live by the faith of the Son of God, who loved me, and gave himself for me.
Galatians 2:20 KJV

Before David walked into his calling, he became destitute and hid in caves. He even lived with the enemy for a season. Joseph was ostracized, and Moses was on the run. Your purpose and destiny will come to life through great adversity. As ironic as it sounds, death produces life. We need to die to our flesh and walk in the spirit. When you walk in the Spirit, you are in tune with God. As you understand this important precept, you will use what God has given you and fulfill your destiny.

CHAPTER 5

PURPOSE MATURES BEFORE YOU DO

Your purpose matures before you actually reach maturity. Esau and Jacob wrestled in their mother's womb because they already knew their purposes. This was so even though they were not even born.

And Isaac intreated the LORD for his wife, because she was barren: and the Lord was intreated of him, and Rebekah his wife conceived. And the children struggled together within her; and she said, If it be so, why am I thus? And she went to enquire of

*the Lord. And the LORD said unto her, Two
nations are in thy womb, and two manner of
people shall be separated from thy bowels;
and the one people shall be stronger than
the other people; and the elder shall serve
the younger. And when her days to be
delivered were fulfilled, behold, there were
twins in her womb. And the first came out
red, all over like an hairy garment; and they
called his name Esau. And after that came
his brother out, and his hand took hold on
Esau's heel; and his name was called Jacob.
Genesis 25:21-26 KJV*

Jesus and John the Baptist were leaping in the womb.
Their spirits recognized the matured purposes within
them. John the Baptist was conceived and born as the
result of a miracle of God. An angel told Zechariah,
John's father, when he and his wife, Elizabeth, came

together God would bless their union and a son would be born. Zechariah doubted the possibility. Nonetheless, God fulfilled His promise and Elizabeth was impregnated with a purpose and destiny through her son, John.

When Mary was pregnant with Jesus, she visited her cousin, Elizabeth. Luke 1:31-45 says that at their greeting, the baby inside Elizabeth's womb leaped and Elizabeth was filled with the Holy Spirit. The baby was so eager to perform his purpose, he began to leap around and dance in his mother's belly.

Your spirit does not need to grow up to know your destiny. You do. All creation is earnestly expecting the manifestation of your destiny. It is as if creation discerns your purpose more than you do. The whole earth is in travail, groaning and waiting for the manifestations of the sons and daughters of God. It is like creation is cheering you on, eagerly waiting for you to hurry and step into your destiny. So hurry up! Read your Bible and pray for guidance!

> *For the word of God is quick, and powerful, and sharper than any two edged sword, piercing even to the dividing asunder of soul and spirit, and of the joints and marrow, and is a discerner of the thoughts and intents of the heart. Hebrews 4:12 KJV*

The soul is where your will, intellect, and emotions reside. The Bible says that God's Word will divide it because, sometimes, your soul gets in the way. Your spirit is already mature because, when you were born, you were full of purpose. Your body needs to wait until your soul grows into maturity and then your spiritual purpose will be released.

Throughout life, you learn things. As you grow into maturity, hopefully you will become a better person. Growing into your maturity is a process that may take a lifetime to achieve. Likewise, your soul needs to mature in Christ and that will take time also.

Think of your soul like a planted seed that needs watering and food daily. By reading the Word, going to church, and watching Christian television, you feed your spirit the nourishment it needs to mature. An example of being immature in spirit is when we complain. I would venture to say that most of us complain at the first drop of bad news that comes our way. A lot of times, we blame God for things that go wrong in our lives. Trials and tribulations are put there to help us mature and grow as Christians. No matter how tough it becomes for you, never blame God and always keep your eyes on the Lord.

God looks at how you act during the low times as well as good times. Though you are full of purpose, your purpose will not be released until you have learned to be a good steward. Being a good steward means that it is your responsibility to make the right decisions in life. Be the solution, not the problem! Jesus told a parable in Chapter 25 of the Book of Matthew about three stewards. The stewards' master had given all three stewards various amounts of talents to care for while he went on a journey.

For the kingdom of heaven is as a man traveling into a far country, who called his own servants, and delivered unto them his goods. And unto one he gave five talents, to another two, and to another one; to every man according to his several ability; and straightway took his journey. Then he that had received the five talents went and traded with the same, and made them other five talents. And likewise he that had received two, he also gained other two. But he that had received one went and digged in the earth, and hid his lord's money. After a long time the lord of those servants cometh, and reckoneth with them. And so he that had received five talents came and brought other five talents, saying, Lord, thou deliveredst unto me five talents: behold, I have gained beside them five talents more. His lord said unto him, Well done, thou good and faithful servant: thou hast been faithful over a few things, I will make thee ruler over many things: enter thou into the joy of thy lord. He also that had received two talents came and said, Lord, thou deliveredst unto me two talents: behold, I have gained two other talents beside them. His lord said unto him,

Well done, good and faithful servant; thou hast been faithful over a few things, I will make thee ruler over many things: enter thou into the joy of thy lord.
Matthew 25:14-23 KJV

To one, the master had been given five talents, another two talents, and the last was given one talent. All doubled their master's money except the steward who had been given just one talent. He hid his talent in the ground because he was afraid. The master told the other two that they had done well and were good and faithful servants. They were then given greater responsibility. The other steward was cast into outer darkness, away from the master because of the steward's misuse of what the master had given the steward. Misusing what God has given you is an example of immaturity.

The Lord will test you. Your real assignment may not have been revealed yet because God wants to see what you do with a small task. This is one reason tithing is important. Once God sees how you handle your stewardship, your purpose and destiny can be revealed. You must be faithful over small tasks in order to be given responsibility over bigger tasks.

Joseph Had To Grow In Maturity

Joseph was a young man when God showed him in a dream that his brothers would bow down to him. God was showing him his destiny. It was several years later before that dream actually came to fruition.

Now Joseph was governor over the land; and it was he who sold to all the people of the land. And Joseph's brothers came and bowed down before him with their faces to earth. Genesis 42:6 NKJV

Joseph was given a vision at age fifteen that prevented him from killing his brothers later in life when they were completely at his mercy. Joseph's brothers were jealous because their father favored Joseph. They were so angry with Joseph because of the dreams he had of them bowing to him, that they sold Joseph into slavery when he was young. Nevertheless, Joseph rose to prominence in Egypt after undergoing many trials, including slavery and prison. Joseph interpreted a dream of Pharaoh that predicted a severe famine after seven years of plenty. Pharaoh then set Joseph over the entire kingdom to ensure there was plenty of food for everyone during the time of lack. The same famine hit the land where his family lived, so Joseph's father, Israel, sent the brothers to Egypt to get food. Joseph was the official with whom they had to bargain. When Joseph saw his brothers who had sold him into slavery, he turned to the side and wept bitterly. Then Joseph wiped his face, turned back to his brothers and revealed himself to them. Immediately, they began to beg and ask Joseph not to kill them. Joseph's maturity is shown in his incredible response:

> *And Joseph said unto his brethren, I am Joseph; doth my father yet live? And his brethren could not answer him; for they were troubled at his presence. And Joseph said unto his brethren, Come near to me, I pray you. And they came near. And he said, I am Joseph your brother, whom ye sold into Egypt. Now therefore be not grieved, nor angry with yourselves, that ye sold me hither: for God did send me before you to preserve life. For these two years hath the famine been in the land: and yet there are five years, in the which there shall be no harvest. And God sent me before you to*

preserve you a posterity in the earth, and to save your lives by a great deliverance. So now it was not you that sent me hither, but God: and he hath made me a father to Pharaoh, and lord of all his house, and a ruler throughout all the land of Egypt. Genesis 45:3-8 KJV

Joseph told his brothers that what they meant for his destruction, God turned it to work for his good so that their generations continue to live. At age fifteen, Joseph would have been too immature to give such a profound statement. In fact, the younger Joseph told his brothers that they would worship him and ask him for things. His brothers thought he was being snotty. So they decided to throw Joseph into the pit. Because of his young age and immaturity, Joseph poorly managed the grace that was on his life.

God had to take Joseph through a process of refining so that Joseph could be a better steward over the call on his life. God needs to bring you to maturity first. Do not give up on your dream or destiny. If Joseph had at any time complained that he was a slave or that he was in prison, then he might not have been in the right place at the right time to fulfill his destiny.

Moses Had To Grow In Maturity

By the time the Israelites had been in Egypt for 450 years, they had become so numerous that Pharaoh decreed that all male babies be killed at birth. Yet, when Moses was born, his mother saw a special grace on him and determined to save his life. She placed Moses in a basket and set it among the reeds on the banks of the Nile River. Pharaoh's daughter went to the river and saw the basket while she was taking a bath and retrieved it. When she saw the babe, feelings for him welled up inside her. Though the baby did not look like her, she chose to keep him as her own and raised him in the palace. Moses spent forty years in Pharaoh's palace and was appointed the next monarch. Remember, Moses was an Israelite raised in an Egyptian house. Yet he knew his heritage. All the while, he struggled with who he was and his ancestry. One day, when Moses saw an Egyptian soldier beating an Israelite, Moses' calling came out of him. Moses was not mature so he did not know how to deal with the calling or understand how God would use him. Therefore, God drew him into the wilderness to perfect the man whom God needed to use.

The Egyptians programmed forty years of Moses' life and now God would manage the next forty years. God perfected Moses in his calling so that Moses could return to Pharaoh and demand the release of the Israelites. Moses did not rely on his fists, a sword, or an army. He relied on God and a rod that God had taught him how to use. He told Pharaoh to let the people go or the water would turn to blood; the sun would go dark; frogs would come from the east, locusts from the west, and lice from every direction; then finally, the first-born would die. Moses' rod represented the hand of God. It was not Moses' power or might but God's power exhibited in Moses. That is why Moses had to go through a maturing process.

God does the same with you. Since you have been walking with God, God has been showing you more. As you mature, God reveals more about you and more about others. The more mature you become, the more God knows He can trust you.

Your Ultimate Purpose

Scripture tells of a blind man who crossed the path of Jesus Christ:

> *And as Jesus passed by, he saw a man which was blind from his birth. And his disciples asked him, saying, Master, who did sin, this man, or his parents, that he was born blind? Jesus answered, Neither hath this man sinned, nor his parents: but that the works of God should be made manifest in him.*
> *John 9:1-3 KJV*

This man was born blind so that God's glory could be manifested when the man was healed. What if the man had been feeling sorry for himself, crying about his blindness and complaining about his physical disability? Would God's glory have been manifested then? Imagine if the man was focused on all his shortcomings and had given the devil an opportunity to destroy his self-esteem? If that had been so, the man would have been at the wrong place at the wrong time and would not have fulfilled his destiny. He would have died blind. This man's ultimate purpose was to bring God glory. His purpose was fulfilled when all who knew him saw him walking with no cane and working instead of begging.

Life for you may have meant having all your bills paid, a big screen TV, suits in your closet, and lizard skin shoes. That is all fine and dandy. God wants you to be successful. But that kind of life is not what I am talking about. I am talking about the life God ordained you to live as it relates to your purpose.

Are you that blind man? Or are you walking around crying and complaining about your shortcomings? Are you feeling sorry for yourself? This behavior will not bring forth your purpose in life. Be like the blind man and walk in the destiny God planned for you. Do not let the devil destroy you at every turn by nagging you and chipping away at your self-esteem!

CHAPTER 6

DIE TO SELF AND BURY THE PAST

Why do you get so angry or become so offended with people? Why does every little thing get on your nerves? The answer is that you are "too alive to your flesh" if you cannot get along with others. You are not dead enough to your flesh if these questions do not convict you. You must die daily and tell yourself that God's Spirit will lead you, not your flesh!

The Bible says you are like a tree planted by the river. God sees the side of you that you are too busy, or too carnal, to see. Bring your flesh under control of the Word of God. This will allow Christ to live in you and be seen through you. You are a walking container of priceless contents.

The story below is about a woman who was desperate in life and how she had to die to self to find life. Jackie hated her life. Every day presented the same problems of where to find something to eat and some place to sleep. Jackie had been on the streets for more than four years. She was scrounging and scraping to stay alive. A failed marriage led to drug abuse and loss of her career. When she graduated high school, Jackie was voted most likely to succeed. "Succeed at what?" she wondered. Jackie felt herself dying more each day. She had no self-esteem and felt utterly hopeless. Jackie felt that part of her had died. Her former life was nothing more than a foggy dream. Some days she wondered if it had happened at all. Then she met Randall. As she was sifting through the contents of a dumpster behind the supermarket, she heard someone call her name. Suspicious that someone was trying to lure her away so they could get all the food, she ignored the voice and kept digging. Again, she heard, "Jackie." Finally, she looked up and saw a man. His name was Randall and he worked at the local homeless shelter. He asked her if she wanted a hot meal and warm bed for the night. Compelled by his kind, gentle nature, she accepted. That was five years ago. During their friendship, Randall introduced Jackie to Jesus. He told her that if she would accept Jesus as her Savior and Lord, her life would change.

Something did change for Jackie. She died to herself and to her past. The failures and abuses that she somehow identified with were dead and buried and her new life has begun. Today, she is clean, well-fed, and happy. She works full time and has no problem making ends meet. Jackie has hope for the future and has found her identity in her destiny as God's child.

There is glory in every one of us. It was put there before we were born. It cannot be bought or earned. We do not deserve it. God said, you may walk in bits of His glory. But you will never walk in the reality of His glory unless you die to your flesh and put your past behind you.

Your Glory And Potential Are Released Through Death Of Self

God said we have treasure housed in a container. What does that mean? Well, one day Jesus shed His "container" when He climbed a mountain and was transfigured into His glorified body. His face began to shine and His countenance became white as snow as two men in their glorified spirits joined Jesus. The book of Luke declares that Elisha and Moses came to Jesus and discussed things with Jesus related to His death. Peter and John witnessed the transfiguration and saw the glory that was inside Jesus.

Each one of us has glory and potential – treasure, priceless contents – inside earthly vessels. Your treasure will only come out through a death.

Jesus tried to explain this to Peter when Jesus said the devil had asked to sift Peter like wheat.

Simon, Simon, Satan has asked to test all of you as a farmer sifts his wheat. I have prayed that you will not lose your faith! Help your brothers be stronger when you come back to me. Luke 22:31-32 CGV

Jesus told Peter that He had prayed for Peter. Jesus

also said after Peter was converted that Peter would strengthen his brothers. Jesus explained that even though a death would take place in Peter, life would come out of it.[a] A death took place in Peter's life and because he died, God's glory began to shine through him. The old Peter would hide, curse, and deny knowing Jesus. However, the Peter in chapter two of the Book of Acts is not the same Peter who existed before God got a hold of him. The new Peter was willing to be locked up in prison and suffer for the Lord's sake. Peter was an apostle who introduced the world to the Holy Spirit on the day of Pentecost.

We Are The Fruit of Jesus' Death

Destiny before identity is the maturing of both stewardship and faithfulness. Death comes before life as it relates to glory. You must die to yourself in order to be able to handle God's glory.

And Jesus answered them, saying, The hour is come, that the Son of man should be glorified. Verily, verily, I say unto you, Except a corn of wheat fall into the ground and die, it abideth alone: but if it die, it bringeth forth much fruit. He that loveth his life shall lose it; and he that hateth his life in this world shall keep it unto life eternal. John 12:23-25 KJV

Jesus was telling a parable about His death. He explained that if He did not die, then there would be no fruit. We are the fruit of Jesus' death. We live because Jesus died. You could say that the corn of wheat came into its destiny. But what if the corn of wheat had a choice and did not want to come into its destiny? What if the wheat did not want to die? The corn of wheat always had the potential to produce a lot of fruit. But only when the corn of wheat dies does it maximize its true potential. Jesus did many signs and miracles in His life. However, Jesus was called to die on the cross and shed His blood so that we might have life. As I stated previously, we do not have to physically die like Jesus did. Jesus had to experience that kind of death in order for the fruit to come. His death was for our lives. There must be a dying of the self before a resurrection of Jesus and a fulfillment of purpose can happen in you. The Bible says the Spirit battles against the flesh and that there is a war, like that of Esau and Jacob, raging in you.

Our sinful selves want what is against the Spirit, and the Spirit wants what is against our sinful selves. The two are against each other, so you cannot do just what you please. Galatians 5:17 CGV

Both flesh and spirit try to get the upper hand. So you

must nail your flesh to the cross before your flesh talks you into pursuing and fantasizing about things God never ordained for your life's destiny.

Starve The Flesh

Paul decided to bring his body under the subjection of the Lordship of Jesus Christ. He decided to starve the flesh. He determined to deprive his flesh of the nutrients it took to keep it alive. Paul vowed to make his flesh suffer because when he suffered with Jesus, he reigned with Jesus. Paul challenged the Colossians to kill the deeds of the flesh.

So put all evil things out of your life: sexual sinning, doing evil, letting evil thoughts control you, wanting things that are evil, and greed. This is really serving a false god.
Colossians 3:5 CGV

The list is not the main focus because no one can write a list long enough to contain all the things a well-fed flesh can do. Adultery and fornication are part of the list. Strife, envy, lust, lasciviousness, and lying are also included on the list. The list is not exhaustive because the flesh never stops. If you let the flesh remain out of control, it will drive men and women to all manner of perversion for sexual gratification. Paul told the church in Rome that what the people had done was so unnatural that God turned them over to a reprobate mind, or worthless thinking, because they refused to kill the flesh.

People did not think it was important to have a true knowledge of God. So God left them and allowed them to have their own worthless thinking and to do things they should not do. Romans 1:28 CGV

God made a deposit in you that you will not recognize as long as your eyes are veiled in flesh. Jesus parted that veil through His death and resurrection, making it possible to see the glory inside. When the Holy Spirit came on Pentecost, the glory of God took up permanent residence in our earthly vessels.

Know ye not that ye are the temple of God, and that the Spirit of God dwelleth in you?
1 Corinthians 3:16 KJV

The glory of God the Father rests in you and me!

CHAPTER 7

FOR EVERY TIME AND PURPOSE THERE IS A SEASON

And He went out from thence, and came into His own country; and His disciples followed Him. And when the Sabbath day was come, he began to teach in the synagogue: and many hearing Him were astonished, saying, From whence hath this man these things? and what wisdom is this, which is given unto Him, that even such mighty works are wrought by his hands? Is not this the carpenter, the son of Mary, the brother of James, and Joseph, and of Judas, and Simon? and are not His sisters here with us? And they were offended at Him. But Jesus said unto them, A prophet is not without honor, but in His own country, and among His own kin, and in His own house. And He could there do no mighty work, save that he laid his hands upon a few sick folk, and healed them. And He marveled because of their unbelief. And He went round about the villages, teaching. And He called unto Him the twelve, and began to send them forth by two and two; and gave them power over unclean spirits. Mark 6:1-7 KJV

Jesus grew up as a normal child, like most other kids. Yet, Jesus was always God. There was nothing distinctly special about Him. He sat with Mary and Joseph, ate with them, laughed with them, worked with them, and cried with them. However, no one knew Jesus was God. In reality, if Jesus were ten years old and sitting by you in a worship service, you probably would not know that this child was sent as the atonement for all our sins. The question is whether Jesus became God at age thirty or whether Jesus was God at age one, seven, or twenty-five? The answer is that Jesus was God from before the foundation of the world. Even in the womb, Jesus was full of grace and truth. Take into account when Elizabeth, John the Baptist's mother, came close to Mary and how Elizabeth's baby leaped in Elizabeth's womb. Jesus' identity was so vague that He was just another Jewish man before He began doing miracles. Nevertheless, Jesus was God.

And the Word became flesh and dwelt among us, and we beheld His glory, the glory as of the only begotten of the Father, full of grace and truth. John bore witness of Him and cried out, saying, "This was He of whom I said, 'He who comes after me is preferred before me, for He was before me.'" And of His fullness we have all received, and grace for grace. For the law was given through Moses, but grace and truth came through Jesus Christ. No one has seen God at any time. The only begotten Son, who is in the bosom of the Father, He has declared Him. John 1:14-18 NKJV

So, what was Jesus doing for thirty years? He was waiting to lay the foundation for His season to begin. A foundation is like a seed you plant, water, and nurture. To illustrate the point, consider an orange tree. When you plant the seed, you expect it will become an orange tree regardless of whether it bears oranges. When its season comes and oranges bloom, there will be no denying that it is an orange tree. But if you do not water it and never give it any plant food, it will either grow to be a sickly tree or it will wither and die. God had to nurture His Son who had to be prepared to spiritually discern to seize the moment. If Jesus had abused His body, He would not have withstood the rigors of His ministry.

God sees you as a tree loaded with fruit. But you may not see it because you are messed up, screwed up, sexed up, and drugged up. What if you were designed to be a famous writer or an artist? You would not want to be missing a hand or be barely able to move because you were in an accident due to foolish or wrong decisions. Your destiny is waiting for you. It is important to be ready to enter it when your season appears. So do not let your season pass you by because you let your body do whatever it wanted to do such as worldly, fleshly, and carnal-minded things. If your body is broken because of self-inflicted abuse, will you be able to do what God is calling you to do? Is there fruit in your life? You will always be that orange tree even if you do not see the fruit. When it becomes your season, you need to be healthy and ready to bear fruit. Likewise, Jesus was always God even though Jesus had to wait for His season to manifest. Another reason that you can miss your season is because of disobedience, carnality and fleshly desires. You are lost because you are messing with this man or that woman, gambling and drinking. You had one foot in the Kingdom and one foot in the world. When your season came, you were pre-occupied and missed it. God does not reveal His glory to lazy people. Do you read the Word and pray daily? Or have your prayed and read the Bible only when you needed something? Your flesh is corrupt and lazy but, as part of the body of Christ, your spirit is born again. So put your body under the subjection to, or control of, the Word. When you listen to the flesh and ignore the Spirit, you will miss your season. I would hate to look back and realize that what God had for me went to someone else because I was lazy!

In the following story, Dylan was going along life's path, doing as little as possible to get by. Dylan was frustrated – again. "Why was that new guy promoted over me?" he wondered. "I've been here longer, I know the job better, and I deserve it." Just as he was going over in his mind all the reasons he should have gotten the promotion, Dylan's boss came over to him. "Dylan, you are probably wondering why Jim was promoted over you. I do not know any other way to say this, but you are just not management material. You take a cigarette break every twenty-five or thirty minutes; you miss at least one and usually two days each week because you are sick or whatever; and you eat constantly at your desk. Look at it. It is a mess!"

"But...but...!" Dylan protested.

Then the pain started. It radiated down his left arm from his chest and shoulder. It felt like his chest was being crushed and he could not breathe. As he collapsed on the floor, he heard his boss shout for someone to call 911.

Dylan's funeral was held on a Tuesday. He was only forty-five years old, but he looked sixty. Too much booze, tobacco, and junk food, his doctor said.

It is very frustrating when your season passes you by because of disobedience or lawlessness. However, it is devastating to miss your season because your life ends early or your body cannot handle the demands put on it. That is what happens when you abuse your body for years. What if your season does not begin until you are eighty years old, like Moses, and you have been filling yourself with barbecued ribs and cheesecake everyday? Eat right! Do not check out before your season checks in! A rebellious lifestyle can negatively affect your destiny. Submitting to authority is not a bad thing. A semblance of order in our lives is a must. We live in a world where there must be rules, otherwise utter chaos would abound.

There are many in the Bible who did not walk in their season. Take King Saul for instance. I imagine he must have felt total frustration when he looked upon his replacement, a little ruddy boy named David. Saul could have remained king had he not allowed his flesh dictate his actions. Saul fought for the accolades of the people, disregarding obedience to God. It cost Saul his destiny.

I do not doubt that every now and then Saul would think of what could have been and, looking upon

David, he could see the same grace that once rested on his life. I am sure Saul saw in David a side of himself that should have materialized. No wonder Saul wanted to kill David. It is important to avoid this kind of situation in your own life. Obey God. And when your season arrives, live it, enjoy it and fulfill it!

And lo a voice from heaven, saying, This is my beloved Son, in whom I am well pleased. Matthew 3:17 KJV

In this passage, God makes it perfectly clear that He is proud of his Son, Jesus. There is nothing confusing in that statement. Regarding your destiny, though, it would be just as nice if God announced from heaven in a loud voice, "Your destiny is that way!" In a way, He does, but not so everyone can hear. God's announcement did not make Jesus the Sone of God.

Also, God did not announce it for Jesus to hear. God announced it so that everyone else could bear witness.

God will also announce your season. Just stay humble and God will speak to your heart about releasing your destiny. You will not have to blow your own horn and you will not need to advertise. God will speak to you about your destiny just as clearly as He announced His approval of Jesus!

If you believe you have missed your season, start praying and training so that you do not make the same mistakes again. Pray that God will be gracious and give you another opportunity to fulfill your destiny. God is capable of doing that!

Your Body Is A Temple

Know ye not that the unrighteous shall not inherit the kingdom of God? Be not deceived: neither fornicators, nor idolaters, nor adulterers, nor effeminate, nor abusers of themselves with mankind, Nor thieves, nor covetous, nor drunkards, nor revilers, nor extortioners, shall inherit the kingdom of God. And such were some of you: but ye are washed, but ye are sanctified, but ye are justified in the name of the Lord Jesus, and by the Spirit of our God. All things are lawful unto me, but all things are not expedient: all things are lawful for me, but I will not be brought under the power of any. Meats for the belly, and the belly for meats: but God shall destroy both it and them. Now the body is not for fornication, but for the

Lord; and the Lord for the body. And God hath both raised up the Lord, and will also raise up us by his own power. Know ye not that your bodies are the members of Christ? Shall I then take the members of Christ, and make them the members of an harlot? God forbid. 1 Corinthians 6:9-15 KJV

Paul says plainly that your body is for the Lord. The Lord needs your body and your body needs the Lord. The Lord needs your body for what He wants to do. If you have you been stuffing the wrong things in your body for years, eating all those donuts, Twinkies®, oatmeal cakes, spareribs and fried food, then you are simply messing with the Lord's temple. When you are twenty, you do not feel the effects of what you eat. However, at age forty, your habits from age twenty will manifest themselves with a vengeance. All the chemicals you have ingested will become apparent and possibly slow you down just as God gets ready to take you into another season.

God does His work through your body. In other words, His work operates through you. Many people are suffering, dying and not fulfilling their destinies because they have abused their bodies and disobeyed God's Word. That is why you should always remember that you are the body of Christ.

For as the body is one, and hath many members, and all the members of that one body, being many, are one body: so also is Christ. For by one Spirit are we all baptized into one body, whether we be Jews or Gentiles? whether we be bond or free; and have been all made to drink into one Spirit.
1 Corinthians 12:12 KJV

We are the body of Christ with many members, functions, purposes, assignments, and talents. Everyone cannot be the head or the foot. We all have our own functions in the body. But, God needs a healthy body to perform His will and carry out His purpose. So exercise and eat well. If we do not take care of our bodies, we do not take care of the Lord.

Unhealthy living can lead to many different kinds of diseases. Cancer is the unrestrained growth of unhealthy cells that usually start growing long before the doctor's diagnosis. AIDS is acquired by the transferring of bodily fluids, often through sexual intercourse. Those two diseases, and many others like them, are the manifestations of an unhealthy lifestyle. Curse the devil and your bad eating habits, alcohol, cigarettes, and illicit sexual activity. Here is a good rule of thumb – before you put anything in your body ask yourself if the Lord would put it in you. Do not end up like Dylan. Everything he thought made him happy ultimately killed him. He checked out before realizing his destiny. Take care of yourself so that you can finish the race and fulfill your purpose.

People Rage When They Cannot Control Your Destiny

And it came to pass, that when Jesus had finished these parables, he departed thence. And when he was come into his own country, he taught them in their synagogue, insomuch that they were astonished, and said, Whence hath this man this wisdom, and these mighty works? Is not this the carpenter's son? is not his mother called Mary? and his brethren, James, and Joseph, and Simon, and Judas? And his sisters, are they not all with us? Whence then hath this man all these things? And they were offended in him. But Jesus said unto them, A prophet is not without honor, save in his own country, and in his own house.

Matthew 13:53-57 KJV

At some time, Jesus went back to the town where He spent his childhood. The reception he encountered was that of dissension, which was partly because the people did not know what to make of Him. Also, no one could take credit for Jesus' wisdom, which was a product of His grace. The people wondered how Jesus, whom they had known from childhood, could make such outlandish claims. Did this man really think He was the Son of God? Jesus' knowledge and boldness angered and offended the people. In fact, the people tried to throw Jesus off a cliff!

Now it happened on one of those days, as He taught the people in the temple and preached the gospel, that the chief priests and the scribes, together with the elders, confronted Him and spoke to Him, saying, "Tell us, by what authority are You doing these things? Or who is he who gave You this authority?" But He answered and said to them, "I also will ask you one thing, and answer Me: The baptism of John - was it from heaven or from men?" And they reasoned among themselves, saying, "If we say, 'from heaven,' He will say, 'Why then did you not believe him?' But if we say, 'From men,' all the people will stone us, for they are persuaded that John was a prophet." So they answered that they did not know where it was from. And Jesus said to them, "Neither will I tell you by what authority I do these things. "

Luke 20:1-8 NKJV

The people could not control Jesus' destiny, so they became enraged. They were looking at His identity as a man. They could not label Jesus or take credit for training Him in school or in seminary. All they saw was the boy who used to play in the road and walk to the town square. He was Mary and Joseph's boy. They could not fathom how He came into His knowledge. By birth, Jesus was not a Pharisee's son, a scribe's son, or a lawyer's son. According to the people, Jesus was just a carpenter's son who was expected to follow in his father's footsteps and become a carpenter.

Many times people will want to direct your destiny for a myriad of reasons. Jealously, unbelief in what you want to do, fear that you may or may not succeed, or lack of faith are some reasons people will want to control your destiny. Do not let them move you to walk outside your destiny. Have faith in God that you will discover, live in, and succeed in your unseen destiny.

Now faith is the substance of things hoped for, the evidence of things not seen.
Hebrews 11:1 NKJV

CHAPTER 8

FINDING THE TREASURE
INSIDE YOURSELF

We are treasures in earthen vessels and those vessels are our human form.

But we have this treasure in earthen vessels, that the excellency of the power may be of God, and not of us. 2 Corinthians 4:7 KJV

God encompasses the universe and there is nothing that God has not created.

***In the beginning God created the heaven
and the earth. Genesis 1:1 KJV***

Everything on earth finds life in God because God is
all knowing. He is the Alpha and Omega, the
beginning and the end. Look to the vastness of the
heavens and God is there. In contrast, look at the
smallest of atoms and God is there as well. Just as the
stars in the heavens are like diamonds sparkling in
the dark firmament, you are like those diamonds.
There is something in you so priceless and so
valuable that money cannot buy it. Everywhere you
go, it is always with you. What is this priceless
commodity? It is God's Glory and Power and Grace
and Anointing. To obtain this priceless commodity,
you must ask God to come into your heart and rule as
Lord and Savior over your life. As soon as you accept
Jesus Christ as your Savior, God can take up
residence in your heart:

Jesus answered and said unto him, If a man love me, he will keep my words: and my Father will love him, and we will come unto him, and make our abode with him.

John 14:23 KJV

When you are born again, you have a treasure inside you, which is Christ, the Hope of Glory. Our God will never leave you nor forsake you. He is always there in the good times and in the bad times. He walks with us, and sometimes, He even carries us. Many times in life, we need to be carried by either God, or someone else, or sometimes by both. When this happens, we need to let God and others pick up the ball and help us run with it. When you let someone else do that, they will receive blessings from God. We have all read and heard about Helen Keller and how she triumphed over her handicap. But did you ever realize what Anne Sullivan, her teacher, did to carry Helen? Anne had to give up much of her life to be Helen's tutor and companion, and Anne did so willingly. Anne Sullivan was a diamond.

Anne was not one to be afraid. But tonight was different. How could she ever make a difference in the life of this child? Anne had been invited to go visit a family whose daughter was "out of control." Blind, deaf, and unable to talk, this seven-year-old girl would be a challenge for anyone, but especially for Anne.

Finally, the two met at the Kellers' house. Just as Anne suspected, the girl had been left to her own devices. Her parents pitied her and were reluctant to bring any discipline. "How could she understand?" was their reasoning. For Anne, though, it was different. Quickly, she began to "spell" words into the palm of the little girl's hand. "She must have a language," said Anne, "for her to ever be successful in this world." Patiently and diligently, Anne worked with the little girl to help her understand the world around her. Finally, the light of understanding burst through the little girl's consciousness. She began to talk through her hands to her teacher and eventually learned how to speak.

Anne Sullivan was a blessing to Helen Keller. It took hard work and perseverance to teach Helen as Anne did not have much to work with, just a few letters tapped into the palm of a young girl who could not see, hear, or speak. But to Helen Keller, Anne was a lifesaver, a life-long companion, and mentor.

What is the treasure hidden inside you? The treasure in you is the Spirit of the living God. It is not your body, flesh or blood. You may take an hour to beautify your flesh. But God looks at your spirit, heart, and destiny. Every person is a spirit that lives in a body. However, not every spirit is born again. Nevertheless, every spirit comes from God and will return to God.

For in him dwelleth all the fulness of the Godhead bodily. And ye are complete in him, which is the head of all principality and power. Colossians 2:9-10 KJV

So once your spirit is born again, you need to look deep inside and see what treasures God has given you. Once you find them, start looking for your destiny and purpose.

Is The Grass Greener On The Other Side?

Ever look at your neighbor's yard and start comparing it to yours? Do you look at what others have and wish you could have it? Or believe God has put nothing in you and brought you here empty? Sounds like you have weeds in your garden. Weeds of jealousy that stem from comparing yourself to others. And what do weeds do? They make your crops become stagnant and slowly they start to decay. God says, "stop looking at other people and see what I put in you." Christians today spend too much time comparing themselves to each other. This sin is pervasive in the church and leads to envy and jealousy. God has given you treasures that are priceless. Stop complaining about what you do not have and start praising God for what you do have. Pastors are not immune to this. They get into competition and try to mimic others, especially if someone's ministry is thriving. They think, "if I just say this or that all of sudden I will be T.D. Jakes." The irony is you cannot work his stuff. You have to work in the grace God gave you. Do not mimic

Benny Hinn because you cannot get to the level of Benny Hinn's ministry by trying to imitate him. He is the farmer of his own seed that he needs to cultivate. It is his responsibility to water and nurture what God has given him. Not yours! Do not steal what God has given another. This is a key point – be your own farmer and cultivate your own land. Then the grass will not be greener on the other side.

I do not have a million-dollar home or drive a Rolls Royce, yet. However, I am cultivating my seed. I have faith and know it is going to happen because I am a diligent farmer. I will not miss my blessing comparing my garden to your garden. I am going to stir whatever God puts in my pot. I am going to work it together and it is going to come out like a cake. It will be different from when it started, and it will develop. However, my crop will never come in if I spend my time comparing myself with another. I am not concerned if your grass is greener than mine. I am focused to use what God gave me to walk in my divine purpose.

A Rod, A Slingshot, A Pot Of Oil, and A Lunch

Moses had a rod. David had a slingshot. The widow had a pot of oil. And a little boy had a lunch. What do all of these things have in common? They were all tools that God used for His greatness. God will use anything He can find to achieve His purpose. Consider how God came to Moses while he was tending sheep on the backside of a desert, or how God came to David while David was in the fields. Consider God's encounter with young Joseph, who was minding his own business. Who were these men? They were no one great. But God does not necessarily *begin* with great men and women. He *makes* great men and women.

In Chapter 3 of the Book of Exodus, God told Moses to go tell Pharaoh of Egypt to let His people go. But Moses told God he could not speak eloquently. Moses was looking at his stuttering problem, but God saw Moses' ability. God was looking at what was in Moses' hand, not what Moses could do with his mouth. God told Moses, "lay down the rod," and the rod turned into a snake. Scripture says Moses jumped back in fear. God knew Moses had a speech impediment, but God told Moses to work with what he had. "Look at what is in your hand, Moses.

Then, whenever you get in trouble, point the rod." Moses did just that. He worked with what he had and pointed his rod at the Red Sea and it parted. He pointed it at the rock and water came out. He pointed the rod at the enemy and the enemy was destroyed.

142

You can bet that Moses probably never left his rod unattended. In fact, for forty years, Moses walked around with this rod, which was his anointing and grace. His destiny was in his hand not in his mouth. God honored what Moses did because he had something in him – the seed of God's purpose.

For years, I walked around with God's anointing and grace on my life but did not know it. Now that I know about the glory and the anointing on my life, there is no way I would go back to drinking Jim Beam and smoking a crack pipe. No way!

David had a slingshot and five smooth small stones. (1 Samuel 17). Those were the tools that God gave him. His brother Eliab told David to put on his armor. But David, being a small boy, could not fit into Eliab's armor because it was much too big and bulky for him. Be careful, otherwise you may like another person's armor that it is not designed for you. So leave it alone. Besides, David knew who he was in God and that he did not need the armor. He had God on his side.

You have your own armor, even though it may not be polished and shining like gold or brass. Do not be afraid of Goliath. Get your little slingshot and let it rip! David reached back and let his slingshot go, killing the giant with one stone. When God empowers you, all it takes is what you already have.

In 2 Kings 4, Elisha ministered to a widow who had no money and whose sons were about to be sold as slaves. When the prophet asked what the widow had in her house, she said, "only a pot of oil." She did not realize that she had a treasure in an earthen vessel. Elisha told her to take what she had and trust God. She took that pot of oil and she found that the oil in her pot was endless until all of her jars were full. Then the prophet told her to go and sell the oil and save her sons. You need to go get some empty vessels and start pouring. God will bless what you already possess. Take stock of your lives, give what you have to God and see what He will do with it.

There was a little boy who was wandering by the crowd. As he looked around, all he could see were thousands of people listening to this man who claimed to be the Messiah. Matthew says in Chapter 14 of the Book of Matthew that they needed to send everyone home because it had been a long day and everyone was very hungry. Jesus asked why they did not just get them some food. Their reply was that they did not have any food, except for a little boy's lunch of five loaves of bread and two fish. Jesus did not complain because of lack. Instead, Jesus told the disciples to bring to Him the boy's lunch. Jesus took the lunch and lifted it towards heaven. He blessed it, brought it down, and broke it. Then He instructed His disciples to pass it among the people. Those five loaves and two fish fed 5,000 men not counting the women and children.

The offering Jesus lifted up and dedicated to God was not the same offering He brought down. Jesus blessed it so much that it came back pressed down, shaken together, and running over. What would have happened if all Jesus did was complain about the little lunch? It would have barely fed five, let alone 5,000 men.

You may only have little to work with at the beginning. Do not let that get in your way. Be like that young boy and give what you have to God, stand back and watch what God does with it. What matters most is that you give your life over to God and then let God to show you the destiny He planned for you.

Is Our Time Up?

We have established throughout this book that God sent you here for a purpose. You have a destiny that God wants you to fulfill. Time is not a factor because God sees time in its completeness. He views the beginning, the middle, and the end of our lives all at once. He knows the end results from the beginning.

Imagine a line drawn on the ground that is six feet long. If you stand on a ladder above the line and look down, you will be able to see the line all at once, from end to end. That is exactly how God sees time and our lives.

So, your age does not matter. It is never too late to find your destiny. God is ready for you to walk into the greatness He has deposited in you.

Do not get sidelined seeing yourself as you are now. God sees where you are going and where you will finish. Go where God's voice guides you. Do not get stuck looking at your past. God does not consult your past to determine your future.

> *And Elisha died, and they buried him. And the bands of the Moabites invaded the land at the coming in of the year. And it came to pass, as they were burying a man, that, behold, they spied a band of men; and they cast the man into the sepulchre of Elisha: and when the man was let down, and touched the bones of Elisha, he revived, and stood up on his feet. 2 Kings 13:20-21 KJV*

Elisha was a prophet so filled with the life of God

that after he died, a dead man who was placed upon Elisha's bones came back to life. What is God saying to you about your purpose in Him? Are you working at your Christianity but not doing what God has called you to do? You seem to be doing all the right things, such as going to church, reading your Bible, praying, surrounding yourself with the right people. But you are not walking in your destiny. First, make sure you are following God's vision, not your vision. Second, do not give up because the real you is about to come out. You may think what you have to offer is small and inadequate, but you are a walking giant. The greatest mistake you can make is to judge yourself by where you are now.

Have you ever bought orange juice? As you know, you can buy it two ways: by the gallon or in a can of concentrate. You are just like the juice concentrate. You are concentrated into your flesh body. All you have to do is mix the right ingredients at the right time, season, and place to reach your purpose. You need to keep pressing forward. Do not waiver and do not doubt God. You could say God has three speeds – slow, slower and slowest. You cannot "out wait" God. What you are today is not everything that God has intended for you.

Someday, you will see the real you. Just like Clark Kent, you will go into a telephone booth one way and come out Superman. Ask yourself this question: "Is Superman always Superman even when he does not have on his Super Suit?" Yes, Superman was always Superman, even in his bathrobe. Hey! Super Christian! It is time for you to put on your Super Suit. Take your mask off. God has spoken over you and no one can change His mind.

He who is the Glory of Israel does not lie or

change his mind; for he is not a man, that
he should change his mind. Numbers 23:19

The seed and its instructions are already in you. Have you ever gone to a home improvement store and seen packets of seed for sale? What is on the front cover of the packet? It is a picture of what those seeds will produce. Each packet has instructions that tell you how much sun the plants need, what kind of nutrients must be in the soil, and how to water the plants. As you follow the instructions, not only will you succeed in your gardening efforts, but you will also succeed in great measure.

The same is true with God. He shows you the picture of what your seed will produce as you follow His directions and walk the path to righteousness.

Because narrow is the gate and difficult is the way which leads to life, and there are few who find it. Matthew 7:14 NKJV

You are not seedless but seed-full. You can rise above anything and any situation because there is something in you to help you overcome. It is called the grace of God. You need to hearken diligently unto His commandments.

And now I plead with you, lady, not as though I wrote a new commandment to you, but that which we have had from the beginning: that we love one another. This is love, that we walk according to His commandments. This is the commandment, that as you have heard from the beginning, you should walk in it. 2 John 5-6 NKJV

Meditate on His law day and night. Hide His word in your heart. Write His Word on the tablet of your heart.

I beseech you therefore, brethren, by the mercies of God, that you present your bodies a living sacrifice, holy, acceptable to God, which is your reasonable service. And do not be conformed to this world, but be transformed by the renewing of your mind, that you may prove what is that good and acceptable and perfect will of God.
Romans 12:1-2 NKJV

You now know that you need to find your destiny that is inside of you. Look at your abilities, talents, and gifts, then feed them the right things. Then let God work your stuff. Remember destiny comes before identity. Find it and catch the vision and go

Zachery Tims

forward. One day, you will stand before Him and you will hear Him say, "Well done My good and faithful servant. You have been faithful with little so I will bless you with more. I will open the door of My warehouse and invite you to enter in."

Do not get used to seeing the same old you, because the one you see here today will not be the same next year. Keep moving on, from glory to glory, forever unfolding. Stand fast in your destiny and your best is yet to come!

154

Free To Be Me

Free To Be Me

THE RELATIONSHIP SERIES

ARE THE RIGHT PEOPLE ON YOUR SHIP?
Audio Set - $20.00

Is there a Jonah on your ship? These messages will teach you how to deal with the baggage of the past so that you can form healthy relationships in the present and future.

WHAT I HAVE IS CONTAGIOUS
Audio Set - $20.00

Have you caught a STD (Spiritually Transferred Demon)? Learn how to replace generational curses and unholy alliances with positive mentorship and friendships.

FRIENDS BEFORE LOVERS
Audio Set - $10.00

If you are single you need this series to teach you how to not become trapped in a relationship that is based on physical attraction and intimacy, but rather develop a relationship based on friendship and communication. If you are married; it's not to late to learn how to repair the gap that becomes obvious when you and your spouse are not in bed! Dr. Tims will teach you how to use Communication, Affection, Recreation, Quality Times, and Intimacy to ensure that you are married to your best friend.

THE MARRIAGE COVENANT
Audio Set - $25.00

We spend so much time planning for a wedding and so little time planning for a marriage. Learn how to reverse the curse of divorce that plagues the American society by applying Godly principles. Whether you are married or single you will benefit from communication tips that Dr. Tims will share in this series. DIVORCE PROOF YOUR MARRIAGE!

Order online at www.ndcc.tv
PO Box 585217 Orlando, FL 32858
1-866-639-3378

The Greek word for "life" is "Zoë." It means having a God-kind of life. Jesus came so that you would have life, and have life more abundantly.